Sales (

Become a Master Closer and Increase Your Sales and Income by Learning How to Always Turn That No into a Yes

Volume 1

By

Income Mastery

competence. There are no scenarios in which the publisher or author of this book can be held responsible for any difficulties or damages that may occur to them after making the information presented here.

In addition, the information on the following pages is intended for informational purposes only and should therefore be regarded as universal. As befits its nature, it is presented without warranty with respect to its prolonged validity or provisional quality. The trademarks mentioned are made without written consent and can in no way be considered as sponsorship of the same.

Table of Contents

Introduction.. 5

Chapter 1: Common objections....................................... 8

Chapter 2: The Need Behind the Need......................... 12

Chapter 3: Negotiations... 16

Chapter 4: The most common mistakes in negotiation.
.... 20

Chapter 5: Preparation... 27

Chapter 6: Objections... 31

Chapter 7: On Closures... 33

Conclusion 37

Exercise 41

Introduction

If you are passionate about the sales and marketing world, perhaps you have already met a customer who is difficult to please when it comes to presenting your product or offering your services. It is common to believe that efficiency, which surely identifies you totally, is a guarantee to close sales and business with potential customers. Many times, believing that doing everything right will lead you directly to success is a mentality that stagnates us and generates frustration when we do not perceive the results we want immediately. In the same way, starting in the sales and trade world can be very intimidating and can generate some mistakes at the pace. the most important thing is to maintain the best attitude in the world and not only have a positive mentality, instead create effective strategies that will allow you to avoid the objections that stand in your way or, in the worst case, learn to manage them and not let them hinder your business.

This book can help you with the possible objections that any client may face to your proposals and you will acquire a basic understanding of them, since understanding the other is the first step to approach him or her, so reflecting on the needs of your clients and why they might reject you will help you to respond assertively and not do so defensively and inefficiently. Furthermore, it is important to understand that an objection can give us enough information to improve the product or actively convince the client, everything depends on our receptivity to the objection and to the words of the other who is refusing, but who is only exposing his most elementary needs.

We must understand that objections are a fundamental element of the daily life of sellers and this has been the case since sales began to position themselves as a professional way from which to receive consistent profits, it has always been so and always will be so, it is part of the job and must be assumed as such. It is impossible to conceive the business of sales without objections, to think this is an unproductive utopia that will not lead to anything good. Behind every objection, there is an opportunity beating and waiting for the seller to take advantage of them. Also, you should think that if your client wasn't directly interested in what you offer, he wouldn't bother to raise objections, that's the introduction to traditional negotiation.

Although to be fair, indeed, the customer is not interested in the product as such, but the benefits it can receive from it, that must be the direction of your speech, so you must orient your words in order to convince him, sales are an art of seduction and, although in personal and sentimental life, objections can be indicators of closed doors, sales are indicators of direction, they show you where you should go and how you should only listen attentively to your customer and translate his words in how to attract him to your product. Don't spend hours and hours trying to explain what the product is, defining it won't help you at all, instead, you should focus on articulating what the product does and its practical advantages about the customer in question, the more specific you can be much better.

From the knowledge acquired in this book you will learn multiple technical and theoretical tools to undertake your way as a seller, all this of course from empathy, ethics, and responsibility. There is no point in blaming the seller for being difficult when it is on your side to have the skills to improve as a salesperson and to assume the responsibilities of such a position.

We hope that the knowledge acquired will change your professional life to the extent that your disposition can be aligned with your talent and your resources for business, you can always give more and believe in yourself is the most important thing. The fact that you are reading this book means that you are looking for information, which speaks well about your personal research. Don't ever stop looking for the lesson you can find in every task you do, everything you are interested in has a method that you can understand and apply, don't leave your future to chance and keep learning.

Chapter 1: Common Objections.

As you know, it is almost impossible to conceive a sale without objections, to believe that it is possible is a fantasy that will not propel us productively towards the fulfillment of our goals. It is likely that if you are already having experience in the sales world, you are already familiar with this reality, there is nothing strange about it and now, we will dissect this reality. Just as there are types of objections, there are types of customers and each one has a particular way of approaching novelty. We have talked to several sellers and service providers and they have shared with us their experiences in the field and what are the most frequent objections in the market.

Many customers often object to the price of a product, this is the most common and the main objection faced by sellers in the business world, often the customer does not have the budget to buy the product you offer, other have it, but considers it excessive. In this case, you must defend the cost of your product or service, explain to the customer why your product costs what it costs, pay attention to the quality of it and how to buy it is not a cost, but an investment that could save him more money in a long term. Of course, it is not ethical to lie, this is simply an approach to such objections, you must argue based on the reality of your product, take the accounts according to the circumstances of your client and expose them calmly.

On the other hand, on many occasions the customer will have objections to the product you're offering, as it does not intend to change the brand you use regularly or simply does not consider your product a priority in their purchase order, perhaps if your customer is a company may have a highly complex protocol when making purchases and you must go through several business filters before closing the sale in question, again this is manageable and it is very possible to manage effectively. Before approaching your client, you should be well informed about how they run their business and make a tentative plan of how your product can improve their already established systems if you know they use another brand, you should go with this previously estimated. Research is the best preparation for a business meeting of this type, if you are prepared you will have the resources to argue any objection to your product, you should always focus this conversation on what your product does or can do for your customer, not on what your product is broadly speaking. The more specific the argument, the further you go as a salesperson.

Also, the client could have a distrust (justified or not) by the product we offer or by the company we represent, could even distrust us as sellers, all this is possible to handle, but undoubtedly the most complicated is to defend us as sellers if the client has a particular conflict on this respective point, as it puts us in a compromising situation where the option of putting us on the defensive is not usually the best basis for a negotiation. It is always easier (and ethical) to defend others who trust our abilities as, say, the company we work for than to defend ourselves. Talking about a company's capacities, its benefits, and recognizing its failures, but turning them as missed opportunities, is much easier than focusing this narrative as a self-defense, in which case you may have to let it go and ask the reasons for the mistrust to better prepare yourself in the future with another client.

It is also important to differentiate between objections that constitute honest doubts of the individual customer or buyer and objections that are excuses for a customer who has already decided not to buy. The doubts and excuses are very different, but both are very natural in the negotiations, both can be handled, but the most important thing is to identify them from the outset.

To begin with, the starting point of any negotiation is preparation. Every seller must go to a highly prepared negotiation, must study very well your product (benefits, strengths, and weaknesses) everything that may be an argument in their favor or against when establishing with a customer. This way you already have a basic preparation that will give you consistent ideas when giving answers in a negotiation dialogue. In the same way, once the conversation with the client has begun, everything you say should come from calm and tranquility, even though you are offering a product, this exhibition should not make you feel exposed or defensive, no matter what the client says, you should never get into controversy, or argue with him or her. Everything is business, nothing is personal equally, you must always be willing to dialogue, even if the client is installed in a monologue, the horizontal invitation to a conversation may be your most powerful weapon.

In fact, when a client makes an objection, what you should do is to directly agree with him, do not doubt it, what he says is always valid, however, this statement is the introduction to your argument and your argument is what you are going to reverse the comment of the client. You are going to give him new information that will be added to his thought, you should not deny his reasoning to minimize it with yours but validate it and then add new knowledge that pretend to seduce him in favor of your product. In this sense, it is a good idea to ask the client more about their objection, i.e., to ask them questions that investigate their reasons, in this way, not only do we receive more information that gives us a clear sense of direction, but we also link up with the client and make a closer and more humane relationship, which is always beneficial in the long term.

As a seller you must be up to the circumstances, in the worst case, the worst possible scenario with a rude or offensive customer, you must be above any comment out of place and always act from the courtesy and respect, so you will never look bad with other potential customers who are witnessing the situation. Once you have established the possibilities of a negotiation, knowing the type of objections you might face will help you prepare better, but we must also understand why these happens in the first place.

Chapter 2: The Need Behind the Need.

It does not hurt to learn a little of marketing psychology in the process of negotiations, after all, negotiations take place between people, so studying the mental processes of the human being when making a decision, can be of great help. Seeing our client as a person at our level is undoubtedly the most effective method, but we must also see it as an entity to study. Reflecting on decision making is important to your position as a salesperson.

When we deal with people, we are not dealing only with what they say they want, but with an entire subtext iceberg that lies beneath their words. In a person's words are hidden influences, unfulfilled desires, secret expectations, personality nuances, prior beliefs and emotional barriers. Historically, people do not buy products for what the product itself is, in each brand or product there is a need behind or an implicit hidden promise, for example, when someone buys a beauty product they are not really aware of every component in it, nor of the cosmetological knowledge of the creators in full, what matters to the buyer is the ability of the product to appeal to his needs, to make clear the promise of a conquered beauty, to prolong the desired youth and increase the stagnant self-esteem, as well as fast food persists in the market because it appeals to the immediacy and indulgence that some customers need from time to time.

Understanding why people do what they do is something any salesperson should strive to understand, but never try to explain. This information will be useful to guide your speech, but it should not be literal. People want to live experiences through products, nothing should be just a product without more, everyone should make those who buy it feel something, because people pay more for how you make them feel, but they would never consider doing so if they believe it is just a product and not a feeling.

When having conversations based on possible negotiations you must know the conversational roles of the clients, which they are:

- The direct.

- The social.

- The reflective.

Now, let's deconstruct every conversational role. The direct client tends to be impatient, determined, goes to the point, does not attend to details and wants to close business quickly, on the other hand, the social client is usually very lively, enjoys the negotiation process, shows interest in his seller as people and, finally, the reflective client takes his time to make decisions, attends and asks for more information about the details, seeks to verify the data and prioritizes the facts before assuming information questionable.

If you perceive that you are dealing with a direct client, you must mimic their way of relating, become a direct seller as well. The best way to do this is to be clear, specific and brief, which will help you to take the points you want to touch and you have noted in a notebook, so as not to be distracted with other topics of conversation that arise at the time. If the customer does not ask for details, do not go into details unless it's absolutely necessary. Try to use words that refer to the effectiveness of the product and give him enough options so that he simply has to choose between the most functional and try to make constant reference to the objectives and results to be obtained.

Also, if you notice that your client is social, give yourself the time to socialize before entering into the matter, try not to be too formal and be friendly when you relate, orientate your arguments from testimonials of other people or other companies, offer personalized benefits, so that they feel taken into account in a special way. In general, these types of customers are people who seek to feel recognized, motivated and inspired in their business interactions. On the other hand, if you have reflective clients you must organize yourself properly, be direct, but not informal, this preparation is extremely important, it's vital, since they will ask you a lot of questions after your exposition and you must be ready to answer them in a clear and precise way. You must give him time to digest the information you tell him and try to use only solid, convincing and verifiable evidence. If you want to get ahead and be the one to give the first point, you can compare your proposal from the start with that of the competition or with the product you know they are using at the moment, this will give you the advantage in negotiation with these customers.

Human beings have basic needs that must be anticipated when dealing with a client. Knowing this will not only help you in business but in your personal life. People have a natural need for personal growth, but also a contribution, security, recognition, variety, and connection with others. Knowing these answers the question: why do we do what we do? understanding your client's real motivation will make your proposals more solid.

Chapter 3: Negotiations.

When we get ready to negotiate, we have to pay attention to our personal image. This is the first step to take care of the other, we must start by seeing ourselves and projecting a neat and careful image. Agenda and commit to PM time and arrive at meetings in AM time, being punctual is also part of the construction of your image. Having visual support is also a big help. The visual is a complex composition, you need to integrate all the elements in a competent image that gives confidence to the customer. It is curious that in fifteen seconds the human mind has an idea of who it is talking to. It is impossible to relate without prejudice, it is almost as impossible as selling without objections, what we need to do is use these instinctive judgments and mold them in our favor.

As a salesperson you have needs that you must evaluate and seek to achieve at all costs, these are usually ego, autonomy as a worker, competitiveness, among other related reasons, however, you should prioritize your needs in relation to the desire for profitability, growth, customer retention, category development, market share and more needs of this type that, in the long term, will make you a better person and a better professional.

We believe that we only do negotiations when it comes to work, but the truth is that this is not true. When two parents are choosing whether to enroll their child in a public or private school, they are making a negotiation and it is a process exactly like what happens in sales, in fact, during courses on negotiations the exercises are usually given around negotiations on every day. Becoming aware of day-to-day negotiations will make you a better salesperson. Knowing yourself as a negotiator is too important before approaching your clients. When we have to wake up early, for example, there is an intimate and personal negotiation, but a negotiation at the end of the day.

Let's think about the children of the house, they are the best negotiators, we can learn a lot from their negotiation strategies. A child never takes no for an answer, may take no for a "not now" and continue the negotiation at another time. If a child asks for candy and his dad says no, the child will keep asking in a thousand different ways until he achieves his goal. Then, the parents will tell him that after lunch he can have his candy and both parties get a benefit from the negotiation. The reality is that the human being is born learned, by nature we already have several very important knowledge for life. Children know how to breathe perfectly (that's why they shout and scream without hurting themselves, they have the ideal tone of voice), they have good posture because they don't have tensions in the body yet and they are natural negotiators. We must relearn all this, learn not to stagnate in positions, but in interests and from there, link up with the other and get what we want.

The children, although it does not seem so, have great levels of ambition and daring, also recognize instinctively that one is not an open door to the commitment of the other party, one is not an invitation to try and so, both parties give a little and give more or less, within their means, but the most important thing about children is their willingness to move forward and not hold a grudge if a does not remain static, their bad memory is fundamental to business as well. Resentment and fear paralyze. To understand that nothing is personal and that there are always new opportunities on the horizon is a mentality that will eventually mobilize us towards the fulfillment of its objectives.

In this sense, it is important that you have strategies when talking with a client. A valid and useful strategy is to do Rapping with him or her, that is, to imitate his or her rhythm when speaking, the tone of voice, to be in tune with your client is something that you can do voluntarily. This happens spontaneously when two people get along, it is normal that when you're trying to get close to someone in a quiet way and this person talks too fast or too loud, because that makes you withdraw unconsciously, on the contrary, if someone is talking enthusiastically about a subject that he is passionate and the other person responds slowly and muted, because they will not understand each other well. See how your receiver speaks, it's not just listening to what he says, but how he says it.

Observation is too important when trying to get to a client, do not forget that our way of processing the experiences of the world is 70% visual, 15% auditory and

15% kinesthetic, keep this in mind and always carries something that the client can see for himself when proposing something. Likewise, you must earn the position of negotiator, since negotiating is a right that you will gain if you fulfill the small promises that will open the way for big projects.

A very common mistake with sellers that are starting, is to start the negotiation by talking about the price and money in between, then the product and the company and there is no space to sell themselves as salespeople, which is highly relevant and few beginning salespeople notice it. If you sell yourself and put your skills on the table, you will gain confidence and ground for a more elastic negotiation that can benefit you.

Now let's talk about how to recognize a good negotiator. A good negotiator radiates empathy, good attitude, warmth, patience, sensitivity and most importantly, practices active listening constantly. A person who is actively listening not only makes his receiver feel included and part of something bigger, but he has the resources and time (during the conversation) to respond based on what the other is saying, so he can be accurate. Good negotiators are patient, innovative, persistent, self-confident, know how to keep calm when under pressure, have flexibility in their way of thinking and acting and are influential in their environment and how it will not be so, a good negotiator has an impact on their context, and everyone notices it.

Chapter 4: The most common mistakes in negotiation.

Negotiation is a matter of adding, never subtracting, much less excluding others. The idea of negotiating is to transform a conflict into a joint problem-solving exercise. There are a lot of motivations that are actually extremely detrimental to our performance as negotiators and gradually make us make mistakes that escalate to ruin our career. For example, wanting to have the reason to look good is something very common when facing a negotiation, wanting to convince another very easily can become two monologues about being right and nothing more. In that sense, we must let go of the desire to appear to have control, appearances are not productive, we must let go of the surface of perfection and go beyond. Winning won't lead to anything if we don't connect with our client, we must keep this in mind.

Our objectives must be oriented towards learning, wanting to learn always puts us in a state of horizontality in relation to our receiver, people feel the pressure even if they do not know they are feeling it, an intuitive prudence is installed in those who feel pressured to accept or do something in particular, if we see each process as a learning opportunity, we will know how to thank each interaction even if we do not close the sale at that moment, we will have made a contact that we can add to a network of contacts that could be useful later in the sales market. Everything is an opportunity and should be used as much as possible. At all times we are relating, even if we do not realize, if we see this that way, we can strengthen our relationships with our customers and put them in value.

Once the reasons have been established, which is very important because purposeless action has an expiry date, we will be able to consider negotiation strategies. First of all, you must take care of yourself, know who you are dealing with to avoid any harm that could be serious, especially when there is money involved. Taking the necessary precautions, you must also be docile to avoid any unnecessary conflict, however, being docile with people is a way to manage your energy, you must be gentle with people, but hard with problems. Take all that aggressiveness and transform it into productive energy, turn the willingness to conflict into impulses to solve problems, this not only speaks very well of you but in reality, is what customers are looking for: someone who solves problems, not someone who is just another problem.

Let's get back to the theme of leaving appearances. Many people believe that sales are about pretending to be erudition and control, but this is false. According to Don Sheeman in his book "Shut up and sell" customers do not want verbiage, do not want someone to dizzy them with words over-explaining, this leads to nothing useful, should talk with pauses that allow the other assimilate the information he is giving, but above all, there are no tricks or shortcuts to negotiate without taking the time to calculate numbers, knowing how much money is talked about when negotiating is vital, there is no way to avoid that, don't try, the only thing you will do is lose money, time and work.

Similarly, care must be taken with closures under pressure or threats, whether implicit or explicit. We all have a threshold of pain, a minimum and a maximum of pain that we are willing to endure, you must have it clear before assuming any negotiation, how much you are willing to lose in a negotiation before giving in, the most important thing is that you have a clear mind not to succumb to external pressures, if you know what your panic zone is, everything that comes before it must mentally prepare you for business. Also, our client has a pain threshold and you should know this, especially when dealing with stated opponents, their ability to change their mind is strictly related to their pain threshold, which you must discover to intervene.

You should also consider the issues to avoid when talking to a customer, there are things you should leave off the table, for example, mocking the competition will not make you look stronger but mean and out of place. Likewise, talking about phobias or fears is frowned upon, you don't have to demean others to look better, but try not to demean yourself voluntarily in any way. The company's problems are another issue that the client should never know about, it will not do any good to "be honest" about problems that only those involved in your company can solve, likewise, religious issues are taboo for these conversations, you should never talk about religion, are sensitive issues that can hurt susceptibilities and create distrust completely unnecessarily, so it is better to avoid them right away, you never know when your client is going through difficult times related to his personal life and religion may arise naturally and you may not know how to handle it later.

Similarly, you must avoid falling into the trap of black or white, phrases such as "we close the deal or I'm going" or "we go ahead or not?", "it's going to be option A or option B," all this closes the options, no one wants to feel that there are no alternatives, never seek to raise a deal like this and do not give in to the pressure of those who propose this type of closures. Actually, this negotiating as if closing a deal was a matter of life or death brings more problems than solutions, we are predisposed to when something matters too much we show the worst part of ourselves, the urgency brings out the worst in people, sometimes we run away, we keep quiet, we talk about more or even attack.

As we said previously when talking about motivations, starting a sale looking to "win" is never a good idea. Sometimes you negotiate with the mentality of a person who wants to win at all costs, involuntarily subdues the other and nobody wants to do business with someone who, unconsciously or not, is demeaning or humiliating you. It is valid to ask ourselves if when one person hits another and these hits are not returned there is a side effect (there always is) and to understand that we should never be the one who hits, we should become aware of this and break these negative patterns. The need to win not only destroys the ego of our client or partners but also violently alienates us from a healthy and productive dialogue.

Another thing that also leads us to unproductive spirals is to go into gossip or tell or hear stories about our customers, attending this kind of thing is a terrible idea because it includes us in judgments and prejudices that do not allow us to relate and know the other for ourselves. When we hear phrases like "I was told that this client was difficult" "he never attends in the evenings" "he is closed" "months ago he told me that he doesn't" and more phrases like that, we must understand that they come from a particular experience of a person who has different ways of understanding the world and relating to people, even if someone tells us in great detail what happened to the client, the words never cover the whole experience, we will never know for sure and the best thing you can do is to focus on your work and ignore the gossip of others.

It is a fact that the buyer has fewer points of reference than the seller, this is normal, and you have to make sure it stays that way. So never stop studying about your field because if the roles change and it is you, the salesperson, who is less informed, you will be at an extremely dangerous disadvantage. The salesman always knows what business he's done. You must fully understand what you are doing, what you did and the implications this has on your profile as a salesperson.

You should know that as a salesperson, you are not alone, you can (and should) rely on a consistent work team, you can go to meetings with an assistant to help ease the pressure of the situation and if you can't sell yourself as an agent of limited authority. Pride will only keep you away from people who could support you in taking your career to the next level. In the same vein, it is important to note that while many people pretend to be wise, pretending ignorance is what is innovative and intelligent. Faking ignorance creates an openness to questions, projects humility, gives curiosity and is a catalyst for important questions. In fact, you have to get used to answering questions with new questions, that's what will give you the information you need to make your point. This pretending ignorance doesn't really mean being ignorant, as we said, preparation is the first and most important step to take when meeting with a client, but you must have this simulation (which is part of the preparation, in the first place) to put the basis of the relationship where you want it to be. Asking your receiver "if you were me, what would I do?" is an excellent way to apply this method, reduces the chances of hasty answers and gives us a more horizontal position concerning our interlocutor.

If you have the opportunity to ask for help honestly, you will be surprised at the result. As I said previously, people have a natural need to contribute and feel connected to others. Amanda Palmer has a TED conference that can easily be found on the Internet where she delves into this subject, is called "The art of asking" and reflects on the real scope of asking for help in a society where recognizing our needs is frowned upon, human nature is even wiser and is above this.

A negotiation is a pact between two parties, this will seem obvious, but it is often very frequent that the commitment to be made is not clear from the beginning, then your buyer goes with someone else who does clarify, people need a call to action that is understandable, ambiguity does not help anyone. Your buyer could give in to this need and the natural pressure of the market and leave with someone else who will tell you exactly what to do. Then, as in a pulse fight, you must clarify the negotiation margins, payment conditions, logistics costs, space profitability, 1% of sales profitability, investment profitability, weight of brands, share in the category, among other issues of this type, only then the sale will be closed with both parties clear of what has just happened, the buyer will be assured that they are on the same page and the call to action will make this pact not only on paper but know how to materialize it effectively.

Chapter 5: Preparation.

We have developed in this book the importance of preparation, we are going to delve into strategies of preparation to negotiate, all this is highly personal and will depend on each person, however, there are general questions that we can all ask before approaching a business conversation of any kind. You can always start by asking yourself What do I want to happen? What is my client afraid of? What does he have? What does he not have? What does he know? What does he not know? What can I give up? This way you can estimate arguments, objections and possible reactions.

Preparing to negotiate is also an exercise in imagination. You can start by writing down on a piece of paper a relevant aspect that you think would be a point of negotiation between you and your client. At this point, agreements must be required, otherwise, it is not relevant for this fiscal year. Now, understanding that there must be a shared purpose in common with your client, you must define the objective you want to achieve in the agreement and then you must propose the proposal and by this I mean that you break down what you want, how you want it, when you want it, why, for what and the same with what you are willing to offer. You can then imagine what the client's possible objections would be and prepare a response for each one.

Think that all of your proposals should be specific, measurable, achievable, realistic, and contemplated within an achievable time horizon. It is necessary to simplify the messages to make them understandable for our receiver, this will make it easier to maintain control of the conversation, something that should be our objective, even though this control is not evident or imperative. At the end of each negotiation, it is important to evaluate the results about the objectives and to reflect on the process, to weigh what worked and what did not work in order to improve each time we have to negotiate with someone new. Also, you think that negotiations do not end in the pact, you have the responsibility to follow up the agreements responsibly in the medium and long term.

Thomas Carlye said that "nothing is worse than activity without understanding", on the other hand, it is true that people make an average of eleven judgments about each other during the first seven seconds of conversation, so you must value the first impression and not forget that your main objective is to make yourself understood, make the client fully understand the goals and objectives you are setting, but above all how you think you can achieve them and what can benefit him to do so.

It also helps if the questions you'll ask your clients are business-related, such as "How's your business? Or questions like what's currently going on in your store? how is the sector (whatever product you're interested in) doing right now? how are sales? what's happened since the last time we saw each other? so if you can actively listen to their answers, the customer will somehow or other tell you what you need to know to convince them, whether they're concerned about costs or profitability, whatever it is, these questions will give you the information you need to detect their real need.

For example, words like "save, need, guarantee, easy, money, results, health, enchant, discovery, security, proven, you / [use the person's name]" are words that will bring you closer to the client, will make you feel confident, will be much more effective than others that, even if it doesn't seem so, blur your attention.

You must also take care of your body language, maintain a good posture, arms without crossing, as well as you should keep your legs without crossing and not have them moving, but have your feet stuck to the floor, you must be planted on the floor to project the security you want. The idea is that you distribute your weight well and have a symmetrical image, which always radiates harmony in the other.

Another foundation of the little-spoken preparation is bodily awareness. Body language can build a good relationship from the first few seconds of presentation. At all times the human being is communicating, even if he is not speaking, in fact, most of the communicational process is not verbal, this is said by many experts in the linguistic area, so we must assume what we communicate with our body and pay attention to what we want to communicate in order to observe how we can fulfill this objective. For example, talking with palms down, seated and balanced projects strength, it seems to say "this is how it is", while palms upward seem to say "help me, I want to please you". On the other hand, a finger pointing forward and moving symmetrically indicates mastery, it seems to say "you will do as I say and as I say", but an asymmetrical body and a sufficiently monotonous tone of voice project reflection and seem to say "I am a reasonable, reflective, logical being. Then, at all times we must keep in mind that our body is our most valuable language and we must make it valid to support our message, not to hinder it.

Chapter 6: Objections.

We could say that everything boils down to preparing ourselves very well in all senses, actively listening, transforming objections into questions, responding with benefits and closing the sale, and then monitoring the business responsibly. Now, we know that not everything is so simple and there are many issues that could complicate the process, however, this process can be thought of in a way accessible to all. It helps if you summarize the analysis of your client's conditions to date with the information you have available, as well as a summary of the conditions you offer and a similar summary of your work as a salesperson or the company you represent, all this to present to the client. You must always attend repeatedly to the key points mentioned by your client, prepare a simple but forceful speech that has the skills to win the interest of your clients.

About your proposal, it must be simple and clear, you must make sure that the client understands very well what you are talking about, you must always satisfy a need and suggest an action to be taken, in addition, you must make sure that your proposal is practical and that it has information that can be translated into a "what is it? Otherwise, it doesn't have much reach in the business world. Always seek to reinforce the benefits to the customer, this is vital, as it will give you the resources to demonstrate that you are satisfying a need. Finally, you must offer options and steps to follow that are easy, nothing too complicated. If your client believes that it is a new problem to change the brand or buy your product, they will not do so if it seems too complex to materialize. The agreement should culminate in an action plan that you will follow very closely to make sure it goes well, it is best if this action plan is accompanied by something that you as a salesperson can do for your customer and not the other way around.

Now that we are coming to the end of this book, we are going to consider a practical exercise that you must do, although it will not be evaluated, the process of writing it and reflecting on it will be of great help to you.

Think of yourself as working for a prestigious company that sells flavored drinks and you find yourself launching a new line of water drinks that are included in a general trend of "healthier lifestyle" and such products. You have three flavors as an option for the public. Now, your buyer handles both types of categories, yet the benefit is that you are working with fruit juices and plain water that, according to previous research, is important to health and is taken into account by the public when buying. You know from the outset that your customer is tough on business, but who wants to be seen as someone who offers the best news on their products. Your ultimate goal is to get space on a standard shelf, that is, two sides for taste, as well as a secondary display. What do you do? Prepare a presentation and discuss it with someone who takes on the role of supervisor.

Chapter 7: On Closures.

We know that closing is too important when doing business, so we must learn how to do it properly, this involves processing some negative extremes of the closures that are frequented in negotiations. Closing a sale sounds like the end of a process and, in part it is, but only in part, we can only say this with reservations, because although a part culminates, is the beginning of a new alliance, so you must make sure that there are no loose ends so that everything runs optimally in the near future.

In fact, every part of the negotiation process can be a close, if you know how to handle it. On the other hand, closing is never the end, it is vital to understand it well. Remember that your credibility is your most important currency, you must manage it as if it were money, this means that you do not intend to force things, over-selling generates a feeling of terrible skepticism in your receiver, which can be extremely harmful to yourself and the product you are looking to sell and, consequently, the company you represent. Whether you are a sales representative or, if you work independently, you are your brand to defend, then acting as such is of great relevance. It is understandable that when you have a great desire to close a sale a sense of urgency arises which drives you to sell with determination, but desperation and determination are not the same they are very different and are projected as such. You must take care of this aspect to ensure a good relationship with the customer and that the closing of the sale takes place in harmony.

In that order of ideas, under-selling is another error, the other side of the same coin, to do this is to go to the other extreme and precisely the most infertile and unproductive extreme. Sub-selling makes it impossible to arouse interest in your customer, plus you don't allow them to evaluate your offer in all its splendor, you fall short and this detracts from the product you're supposed to sell. Try to maintain a balance in your profile as a salesperson, do not go to a level of extreme and terrible urgency, but much less try to overcorrect this by minimizing you and your product. Balance is the best advisor to those who are relating to others, especially if this relationship has money in it and sustains your career.

Some reasons why some sellers do not place an order on time efficiently is because they are afraid to receive a no answer. Fear is paralyzing and puts you in a passive position that is not ideal for any salesperson of any kind, so try to think that fear is your partner, this is the one that should drive you to close the sale, ask for the order and articulate the next steps to follow. It is true that a negative after having done everything right and having invested time and energy (and at this point in professional life we already know that time is always money, so it is a double loss of human and economic capital) but it is better to walk in the light of the truth, at least you already know if that ambiguity was a no and you have a new learning that adds to your work experience.

You must accept at the outset that you will never know what the buyer is thinking, so assuming it will only drive you crazy and prevent you from taking the lead in the professional field that concerns you. Just connect with him as if it were not something of life or death, project security and everything will be fine. In the same way, to think that your client has not completely understood the subject and there are things to explain makes you prolong the interaction and this elasticity may not play in your favor, you must be as clear as possible and economize your words intelligently, be simple, but precise. If you prepare well enough, you will have the resources to make a brief and efficient presentation without too much verbosity, but if you think you need to talk hours and hours or have thousands of meetings to close a case, it is true that your client may be very hard, but also think that your previous investigation may have affected you, since if you had the necessary information you would have already hit the nail on the head with what the client needs to make the decision. Remember that time is money and no one wants to waste either of these two valuable resources. Stretching the time to give the order does not do your company, you, or your client a favor. Trust yourself and leap before you lose time or miss an opportunity to bore the customer with meaningless talk or no clear direction.

On the contrary, feeling that your client has all the necessary information too soon and that you don't need to ask, will only generate too uncomfortable situations that you will be discarded immediately. Indeed, you do not want to delay an interaction unnecessarily, but neither should you rush into something that is not yet complete. Again, balance is ideal and you must create a solid criterion to detect when it is time to give the order and establish the steps to follow for each of the parts. The latter is also vital, when you already have the criteria to ensure the timing of the order, you must give a viable action plan, which means you must have it prepared and estimated beforehand, you must have all possible resources to carry it out and know that your client also has them to do their part, otherwise it will also be a waste of time and energy, besides being extremely frustrating for both and a lousy way to finish something that could have been a wonderful strategic and functional business alliance to maintain over time. So, you must always seek balance and have a solid foundation of preparation, research and, above all, self-confidence. If you trust your preparation and your abilities, you will be able to achieve any business and any goal in your life.

Conclusion

Now that we have reached the end of this book, we hope that all the knowledge received from it will be useful for your future, but we must not forget your personal life, which we hope will also benefit from your new negotiation and objection handling tools. As we said previously, the human being is an excellent negotiator by nature, but the sentimental education we receive often kills our instincts to get what we want. It is important to remember that all those resources are already within us, we just have to relearn them, we must remember them and give them a life of their own.

We must also remember that, while it is true that we are always in negotiations with others (our clients, bosses, relatives, partners, children, etc.) we are also constantly in negotiations with ourselves. We are our most difficult negotiator to carry, we cannot see ourselves from the outside and therefore, we do not judge ourselves. Whenever we have to be punctual and find ourselves in the difficulty of sacrificing something to properly manage our time and achieve our goals, we are managing the objections we set ourselves to achieve short-term gains above our long-term goals. For example, when we have the option of a recreational social interaction, but it will take away hours of sleep and rest necessary to work optimally the next day or when we must sacrifice those hours of sleep to prepare for an important presentation of work, all those cases are moments in which we divide and we do the roles of client and negotiator, we present the objections and we must clarify our real needs to convince ourselves to do what suits us best in time.

Being clear about the strategies you use with others, but applying them to yourself will give you the perspective you need to achieve your goals and cut terrible patterns of self-sabotage that at other times may have ruined great opportunities, after all, you are solely responsible for your happiness and it is probably you who stands in the way of your greatest goals.

In the same way, as you monitor your projects, you should monitor your wishes and goals. It is always important to ask yourself why you want to do what you dream of, listen to your motivations and attend to those objectives, your purpose is what will mobilize or paralyze you, depending on its strength and how deep-rooted it is. Sometimes it's tragic to grow up far from your goals, changing your dreams is changing your destiny and is closely linked to who you are as a person. Recognizing that you are no longer the same and want something different is key to stop wasting time and undertake your new goals. Whenever recognizing your change does not imply avoiding the path that materializes with sacrifice and work, but an honest observation of your present, do not forget that it is relatively easy to lie to your partner, your companions, your friends, but lying to yourself is terrible, beyond being sad, it is unproductive, it is a lie without reach that will lead you to nothing eventually, it will only make you unhappy and will leave you in a static and sterile future. If your goals are clear in your life and you already know what you want, as well as when you close a sale and establish an action plan with your client, you must identify the actions to be taken to achieve your dreams.

Some experts agree that making to-do lists (especially when they have to do with personal goals) can be overwhelming, which can lead you to do nothing at all. In these cases, they recommend making lists of things done and start there, that is, change those "To do list" by "To did list/To-do list" and integrate what has been done with what remains to be done, so you can observe the road traveled and understand that each step has taken you to where you are, so your desires will not seem impossible because you will always have in perspective what you have already achieved and taken for granted. This can be extrapolated to your professional life, sometimes when a client seems too difficult, writing down on a piece of paper the deals you have closed or everything your company has achieved and how this could benefit your recipient, will be very helpful, not only keep it in mind, but in fact write it down on paper, as experts in the field also say that we process information better when we write it down, somehow we manage to internalize it. So these statements that are not based on good wishes, but on facts already confirmed, will have a real impact on your psyche and your immediate reality.

Now that the book is coming to an end, I would not like to close without first leaving one last exercise as the closing of this learning process. Feel free to do it or not, but you must know that doing it will be useful to metabolize all this new knowledge and is an exercise that, even if you do not do it right now, because it does require time to do it in its entirety, you can return to it when you need it for work purposes. Then find a place to score and let's get started.

Exercise

Get two or three co-workers, preferably people you work with or who are in the same industry as you, take an hour to prepare a preparation for a buyer (they must first establish a narrative about who the buyer is and the circumstances are given, it helps if this is real and someone you'd really like to work with). Next, establish an initiative and a real sales problem, for example, there is a new product that has unfortunately been found to be out of stock during the last two visits. It has a very bad placement of space on the shelf and they want to solve it with a new promotional exhibition. They have to make a five- or ten-minute presentation.

Establishing guidelines and having people to respond with, as well as practicing your speaking techniques, is extremely important because you have someone to try strategies with, without the pressure of real closure, so when the time comes you'll feel more comfortable and be able to relate to better preparation which, as you know, is the wisest trick in the world. The better prepared you are, the more trust you will have and people smell trust as much as dogs smell fear.

We hope that everything you have read in this book will be of great help to you and give you the resources you need to improve your relationship with your clients' objections, however, those resources are already in you, you just have to find that natural negotiating strength within you.

Lightning Source UK Ltd.
Milton Keynes UK
UKHW022109281222
414549UK00018B/177